AUTISTIC REFLECTIONS
IN A STEEL MIRROR
REFLECTED

FELIX NEALS

AUTISTIC REFLECTIONS
IN A STEEL MIRROR
REFLECTED

ISBN: 978-0999039311.

Cover Design by **JACOB VU**.

TRIBUTES

To the many: Families who underwrote my life: Neals, Wilson, Harris, Johnson, Martin, Kincade, Nelson, Leong; people who shepherded me through mazes of knowledge in the institutions – Stanton School, US Army, Idaho State University, Washburn University School of Law, Menninger Foundation, New York State government. I am very grateful.

Thank you.

Felix.

fneals@gmail.com

THE AUTHOR.

Felix Neals, a retired New York State civil servant, worked in various jobs: Attorney, Office of Economic Opportunity; administrative law judge; supervising administrative law judge and special deputy secretary of state, Department of State. Before government service, Felix worked for ITT (NY, NJ), attorney and administrator of education; and for RCA (NY, Palo Alto) administrator early-education computer applications a joint venture with Dr. Patrick Suppes, Stanford University, Institute for Mathematical Research in the Social Sciences.

Born in Jacksonville and reared in both Jacksonville and Miami, Florida, Felix, during his childhood, was referred to as "mentally slow" by the public and was explained as "touched" and "different" by his family. In the racially segregated communities in which he lived, there were few educational and medical resources. His childhood was deriding, his early education derisive, and his mental health care indigenous.

Felix enlisted in military service at an underage. He served in racially segregated, US Army units, faced summary court-martial and demotion in rank from sergeant to corporal. After a honorable discharge (WW II veteran, Pacific Theater), he earned a B.S. from Idaho State University, won a U.S. National Intercollegiate Oratory Championship, was selected to Who's Who Among Students in American Universities and Colleges, was awarded the Degree of Special Distinction in Pi Kappa Delta Honor Society, and was chosen a finalist in an annual competition of Yale University Series of

iv

Younger Poets. Felix obtained a J.D. from Washburn University School of Law, Topeka, Kansas. In Topeka at the Menninger Foundation, Felix, an employee and outpatient, first learned of "autism." Prior psychiatric diagnoses of "mental retardation" and "schizophrenia" in his life were displaced by the word, "autism," at that time, a relatively new medical categorization. He describes the era in his life before "autism" as "knowledge delayed, treatment unknown, behavior ordained."

Felix's memberships included state and national administrative law judge associations. His writings include Articles on Psychosystematics: (Felix's method of forging conceptual mental networks to subjugate autism to his life); a law book, *New York Administrative Law, Executive Agencies, and the Administrative Law Judiciary*; a book of essays, short stories, and poetry, *Autism in Black Matter.*

CONTENTS

Black Rose.

The black rose,
window-boxed and wind-lashed,
beats against
the picture window pane.

Remnants
of black matter
stick to glass;
rouge-red reflects
across chiaroscuro.

Rage flares soundlessly
in violet tones
on colorless bodies
of solid hate cheering
dramatized idiocy.

Madness tints the lips
of native faces
with *faint-hysteria*
in stunning blood.

TODAY'S TOMORROW.

Today ends.
An irreversible paper yesterday,
ripped from my calendar
and throw into today's trash,
burns and turns
into irrevocable ash,
vacates a place
to make a place
for today's tomorrow.

I sit, gather hot embers
on my naked lap, and rock;
plenary winds rise
in virtual freedom,
fan smoke and ash,
and toss torched time
into visible reality.

Affixed to the earth,
I look to the sky and see
smoke and ash fleeing today.
I jump into fragments
too heavy, as I, to fly,
and hide here between
tomorrow 's yesterday
and today's tomorrow.

2

ROTATION.

We swing our words
as verbal hammers.
Among the splinters
of brittle trusts
and fragile faiths,
we seize every advantage –
be it a bad piece of probity
or in the form of a profane fate.

Our finished actions,
our spoken words
lay upon the fireplace mantel
among other aboriginal relics
encircling the antique clock,
yields of old exchanges
varnished by vintage quarrels
and exhibited villainously
for viewing and evocation.

We wind the antique clock;
it unwinds; we rewind
the unwound;
the rewind unwinds.
Repetitious, evocative sounds
resound in relentless releases.
The seconds tick-tock;
the hours ding-dong;
the mantel vibrates;
the relics shake;
We rotate.

WILLPOWER.

Data knocks
at a blindsight door
in the brain.
Membrane vibrates;
consciousness awakes
and expands my view
to detect and to define
the data at the door –
A truth or a threat?

I scan the information
across thought and function;
concurrently, I apply reason
counterclockwise and clockwise,
pass insight and foresight
through conception.

A message of truth,
focused to fit any function
in brain or of mind,
advocates a change
in brain and of mind
and threatens to compel
a change in me.

Subconscious, unconscious,
and conscious combine
into the strength of mind
to bar the door,
prevent an emotional coup,
and preserve the unique identity
of an ever-changing me

4

defined and systematized
by an ever-changing mind
integrated and regulated
by an ever-changing brain
folded, floating and imprisoned
in an imprisoned me.

HAPPY NEW YEAR.

Again,
the tentacles of the clock
move right,
push the final second
of this year to midnight
and into the quicksand
of abstraction.
History sucks off last year.
In the orgasmic aftermath,
revelation leaks one drop of life
upon the new promise
to you, me, us.
Again.
Happy New Year.

CEREMONY OF PAIN AND PLEASURE:
RITE OF PASSAGE
(Three Phases).

I.
My rite of passage
to revelation to fix
my being begins:
I breathe deeply as I step
over the doorsill of docility
and into the hammering rain.

Iron clappers
strike iron sound-bows;
peals of bells reverberate
in tones that hunt
for a place among tones
rapidly decaying in vibrations
of echoing tunes.

The sounds of bells and rain
incant my leaving and break
my isolated aloneness
into pieces.

Purpose mixes with rain
and washes me as I walk warily
along this path of circumstances
of the park, pass stalks that protrude
from a sodden earth and point
wet sunflowers toward an unseen sun.

The Easter lily I carry bows
majestically from the weight

of a baptism in rainwater.
"Mother!" Amused children call.
"Look at the silly man!"
Children sense my silent ritual
to keep my consciousness conscious.

I make many paper boats.
Fragility and mastery show
as each fashioned page floats
upon waters in tubs.
The wind is the breath
I blow wearily, ever so wearily,
in my customized captivity.
Decision tilts; indecision sinks
and tears the pulpy paper strips
that anchor me to the shore
of social piers.

Crouched in infantile conduct,
I follow laughing children
who follow buoyant things
along a gutter's stream
to a sewer where the things
sink and the children scream.

The salutation to sewage
heralds my arrive at my destination,
the sacred site of the church.
The door to ceremony,
closed and locked, bears
a purple-lettered sign:

The Law of the Church.
Easter Services celebrate
the discipline of religious werewolves.

8

Admission by invitation only.

II.
I break down the church door,
enter the sacred place,
and walk to the altar
in strides that pulsate
in rhythms of my being.
I reek of the aromas
of my public orientation,
epitomized in the werewolves' eyes:

Crazy, dumb, stupid,
uninvited,
touched;
take a pick!

I take the pick of the litter,
"Touched."
The chosen wags its tail;
it smiles; I smile.
My smile dances among the smiles
stowed within my lips
for public use in private causes.

"I interrupt to introduce myself
with a word that's both
a symbol and a sign:
I am 'Touched.'
I am here to testify before witnesses
to free me from testimony
and from need of a witness.

"I renounce the symbol and the sign.

Neither identifies or designates me.
I repudiate the word's
explanation of me
as a symbol of omission
or its description of me
as a sign of commission
in a human condition.

"I reject the word's mystical affair
with the need of others to use
the word to portray my humanity
by programming my immediacy
with predicted experience.
I find immediate experience
pure, absolute and real,
the natural state
of the truthful existence
of the experience experienced.

"To diffuse the word,
I must infuse the word,
break the rigor mortis
in the sign's definition
and mummify the symbol.
I must infiltrate
the experience of being."

On the altar, I burn the Easter lily
in fire fed by pages torn
from bibles and books of hymns.

III.
Wind enter through
the broken door, whirl and twist

around me into a vacuum,
uplift the burnt offering,
and immerse me
in smoke, cinders, and embers.

Pure, absolute, and real,
I laugh and hum
and watch the werewolves
watch me transform.

Relativity.

The place beyond space
and the place between spaces,
are spaceless places.

The space beyond place
and the space between places
are placeless spaces.

Spaceless places and placeless spaces
space places and place spaces.
Place and space without separation –
a space in a place and a place in a space.

Space place, place space –
Instantaneous
synonymous
infinities.

NIGHT OUT.

We stepped out of the theater,
and without a word or a look,
you took my hand.
We both shook in release
from the play's probe
and felt an avid void
when we reached the spot
where the lobby and the street meet.

Grip my hand tighter, please.
Let us be unafraid
of the experiences
our hands have had.

We could not afford tonight's happiness.
They could tell at the barbecue pit,
the way we looked for and found
the precise amount of coins
to pay in change for a pound of ribs.

Change. The change we became
for an evening we relinquish
and return to the tenement
that we do not become.

We are almost home. Just past
the store-front restaurants
wherein fast-foods
quickly served in foam
are abruptly devoured
with plastic, and wherein
parsimonious eyes

reconnoiter the sidewalk,
scan the pages of books
gossiping about concepts of ages,
and prowl in the last sheets of newspapers;
there, the eyes march like troops in slow time
through installment plans, the new and the used,
positions, pensions, low-interest loans,
rewards for correlations, and funeral parlors
promoting family-sized burial plots
and pre-inscribed tombstones.

Walk slower, please.
Do not turn right at the corner.
We could turn left,
choose a selfish future
for just one more hour.

There are so few bones in a pound of ribs.

Even before I look up
at your face, I know your answer.
Love and understanding
are featured there.

We shall turn right at the corner,
climb the many steps, unlock the door.
The largest child will be proud
of the order that she has kept;
the smallest child will crawl
across the floor, pull at my skirt,
expect a present – not being tired
of receiving and not having
learned to give.

We will not eat, and with a smile,

we shall serve each child a bone.
You will divide the bones
into impartial parts without need
of a scale; in fact, you could do it
by touch alone. Your fingers' performance
testify to the forced practice of years.

Don't forget to save a bone
for our little leaguer at the game!
And we shall have a game at home,
one you will invent to cover
the embarrassment
of "not-enough."

What shall we name the game tonight?

Perhaps, instead, we should compose
a song to sing to soften the sound
of small teeth gnawing on a bone.

There are so few bones in a pound of ribs.

HISTORY.

History.
Explore history.
Enjoy historians'
use of opinion,
interpretation,
and explanation
to give sight and sound
to antiquity.

History,
neither an instructor nor a predictor,
is, at least, a confused courier of events;
is, at best, a chameleon of memory;
is, at worse, a marauder.

History's
mendacious fingers
should not be trusted
to revive the heart
or to rescue the mind.

History's
version of a vision
does no more
than it should –
Entertain.

PERPETUITY.

In the afternoon,
an intermittent hum
whizzes past my ear,
a bizarre and puzzling noise
from an unknown location
traveling at an unknown alacrity.

Clarification zips in,
carried on the four wings
of a honey bee;
it performs a tremble dance,
stings me, injects
two barbed lancets
into my face,
falls, and dies.

Tears from my pain,
blur my sight
at the moment
of the honey bee's death,
at the moment
of my blind surprise!
I see the reason:
Flights of life-and-death
move in perpetual plights
among moments;

life and death,
separated conceptually
at conception,
turn, face, and embrace
conceptually

and instantiate
the property right
of essence – the eternal gift
to exist exclusively
in private consciousnesses.

IDENTITY.

What you do
and why you do
what you do
when and how
you do what you do
as you do it to me,
I feel without need
to do to you.

Who you are
and who you say you are,
and what you are,
and what you say you are,
as you say it to me,
I listen without need
to say to you
what you say to me.

Who I am
and who you tell me I am,
and what I am,
and what you tell me I am
as you tell it to me,
I hear without need
to tell you
what you tell me.

I ignore the terror
you eulogize,
erase the error
you validate,
and nail corrections

over your lies.

I look into your eyes
and see without need
to authenticate
or to correlate

who and what you are
and who and what I am.

REALITY OF ILLUSION.

To be real
where I am when I am where I am,
I conceive, perceive, and believe
I am where I am when I am where I am
in the illusion of the reality
in the illusion of existence.

I am real
where I am when I am where I am
in conceived, perceived, and believed illusions
of illusions conceived, perceived, and believed.
I conceive, perceive, and believe
I touch me,
you touch me,
we touch me
in my conceived, perceived, and believed
reality.

NEUROTIC BALANCE.

Using very little space
at the end of the couch,
I sit and wait tolerantly for you
to perform today's psycho-drama.
You do it so well.
What fret will you enact tonight
as you get lost in feelings?
You exhale loudly;
you are ready to begin.
This time, as every time,
your abstract anger causes
idiosyncratic absurdities.
You grumble about secret faults,
yours first to underpin
your renovation of rebuffs
and misunderstandings.
You reassess and reflect
on experience as weakness;
you confront comment
as allegation or accusation
that indicts you as both
victim and vanquisher.
You agonize; I dispassionate.
You involved; I uninvolved.
You impractical; I pragmatic.
You disbelieve; I disregard.
You suspicious; I indifferent.
You reject; I tolerate.
We indivisible.

STRANGERS STILL.

I look at you looking at me
not seeing you not seeing me.
Not knowing what you see
or how you see what you see,
I do not know if I see
as you see.
I think not.

I listen to you listening to me
not hearing you not hearing me.
Not knowing what you hear,
or how you hear what you hear,
I do not know if I hear
as you hear.
I think not.

I touch you touching me
not feeling you not feeling me.
Not knowing what you feel
or how you feel what you feel,
I do not know if I feel
as you feel.
I think not.

We are as we are called –
Daughter, son, wife, husband,
mother, father, mama, papa –
Strangers still.

PEOPLE.

Now is how it is some time,
now that sometimes
there is some understanding
of "us, 'those people,' "
by "those, 'those people.' "

Now is how it is some time,
now that sometimes
there is some understanding
of "those, 'those people,' "
by "us, 'those people.' "

Now is how it is some time,
now that sometimes,
there is some understanding
of "those, 'those people,' "
and of "us, 'those people, "
by "we, 'the people.' "

Now is how it is some time,
now, that sometimes,
there is some understanding
that "us, 'those people,' "
and "we, 'those people' "
are "people."

QUINTESSENCE.

I did not feel the orbiting world
turn the warm Kansas night
toward a deep star
to align with an arctic wind;
nor did I see the moon change,
but I was told that it became oblique.

Perhaps while still asleep,
I felt frost enamel the spring air;
when I awakened, there were covers
uncustomarily about my head.

During the night, I heard things fall
and though they to be rain
until the cold morning's bright sun rose
and revealed thousands of green leaves
dropping from trees
to a glaze of green
topping the terrain
farther than my sight.

Verdant death on the sand
enters rot's routine of decay
through declensions of colors –
new green on grit, down to
new dust in dirt, down to
new growth in old ground, down to
a voracious digestion
of immortal matter, down to
the quintessence of
continual energy.

POLITICS.

While you're on your feet, Little One,
do me a favor, won't you, Hon?
Bring me a cup of coffee, please.
Oh, and a slice of toast with cheese.
Gee, thanks an awful lot.
Oh, heck! Would you wipe up that spot?
Thanks. Say, how long before you'll be coming back?
Well, bring me a cigarette – no, make it a pack.
Thanks. May as well get an ash tray
since you're going that way.
Huh? Oh, I have one. You didn't look
over here. Hand me that red book.
Thanks. Hey! Switch on the light.
Wait! It's Saturday. Get the fight.
Gosh, it's cold in here.
Turn up the heat, would'ya, Dear?
What was that? Someone at the door? Better see.
Oh, it is the paper. Well, give it to me.
What? Something else before you take a seat?
Well, since you're on your feet.

GHOST.

Funerals are held in afternoons.
We said our final goodbye
as lovers at night.

That night was to be and was our goodbye.
When I arrived, your hope was showing.
You welcomed me and casually bolted
the door, locking the inside-us in
and the outside-them out.

I knew it was the you-in-you
peeking through the me-in-you (again),
trying to commit the me-in-you (again)
to the you-in-me and tag tomorrows
"ours." The merciful me-in-me
broke out of the merciless me-in-me
to let the you-in-you
get free of the me-in-you.
You cried,
"Goodbye."

You died.
Free of the me-in-you,
you left the ghost
of you in me.
I cried,
"Hello."

PASSION.

Mind filled with thoughts
of soft blending dimensions
silhouetting your hollows,
curves, and lines, we sit here,
my passion and I, curious
about the caverns
of your emotions.

My hands lie still
while my eyes hug you.
My passion observes and yawns.
I feel no surprise;
it yawns often lately and sleeps,
perhaps looking for a dream
in which to be satisfied.

To be kind, I whisper to my passion,
"Darling, goodbye."
It yawns again and smiles.
It sits on my lap and nods.
I start to shake,
anticipating its sleep.

I do not like the sleep-sounds it makes
nor the way it sleep-crawls
in and out of my emotions.
And when it awakes,
I do not like the way
it says grace, calls your name,
and dines on my heart.

But most of all, I do not like

the way, after eating,
it washes its lips
in my blood.

I feel so cold.

FIRST MEETING.

Frequently, at a first meeting,
ears hear but do not listen,
eyes see but do not observe,
hands touch but do not feel,
lips brush but do not meet,
arms enfold but do not hold,
and words are spoken as verbs.

Our first meeting, I recall.
We shook hands.
We questioned and answered,
looked and commented.
You read my palm.
We danced slowly and swiftly.
We spoke our words
in the form of pronouns.
We kissed farewell
at our first meeting,
our last.

GARDEN OF LITERATURE.

A word expressed
always exists
in isolation,
a brief interlude
in time and space,
a single element of a conception
circumscribed in silence or sound.

A word fitted with
individually selected words
formulate phases,
clauses, and sentences
into worded consequences.

Words shelter life.
Life lives in a world of words –
common words; violent words;
counterfeit words; conceiving, deceiving,
receiving, and perceiving words.

Words trapped within thought
extend into elongated words,
mate with words of action,
inject words into words
and spawn words.

Progenies of words
copy, clone, consign, cycle,
and grow words into
gardens of literature.

NOISE IN THE FIELD.

We vary about the noise in the field.
The specter of extremes slips between us,
and we rearrange the blankets to make a place
for the guest of discord. Therapeutically,
we should get up and dress,
leave the grace of bed, indulge a must,
let our eyes explain – record a party or a riot,
narrow at a wrong, widen at a right.
But there is no need for rising;
with the crossing of my eyes,
I can summon the view on the field
to the cervix of space
between the curtain
and the window sill
and shall describe:

Soaked shadows
trip over raindrops,
tumble into apparitions,
obscure vision, and distort reality.

Thunderbolts fracture air;
eventide and rainfall collide,
merge with nightfall, freeze,
and drop onto the frozen field.
Cracking ice booms
as ice quakes announce
climate change.

It was the collapse
of the arrival
that we heard.

CONSEQUENTIALISM.

Often I speak of virtue,
and just as often,
I evaluate my actions
with vague utilitarianism
and obscure the light
of virtue's rare
revelations.

Hereafter, I shall vigilantly
aggregate the values of virtue,
highlight the ethicality
of virtue, and validate
the light in virtue.

Hereafter, I shall come and go,
give and accept,
and act and react
always in the light
of virtue's
consequentialism.

Hereafter, I will.

STREET BEGGAR.

Words chanting ambiguous hurts,
words wearing rag-covered needs,
words hurled against passing flesh
resonate the drag of broken feet
by a big and broken man
over the broken street.

Words stained, words coiled,
words wrapping mangled limbs
extend grief in rhymes to strangers.

Words begging, words prostituting,
words with hard heels click
in quick tautological tunes
of the beggar's stick
tapping against brick.

Metal money tossed
into the tin cup
strikes bottom
with the metallic response
of alms ricocheting
in foraging footnotes
to the beggar's riposte,
"Thank you. God bless you."

ORGAN DONOR.

The card asks, "What is donated?"
The answer, "All. Take all of me.

"The eyes view Hawaii,
the heart beat in California,
the liver taste the water in Saratoga,
the lungs warm the air in Alaska.

"The bones rouse the imagination
of students in an Idaho science class
when a six-foot-six-inch skeleton
rattles in a torrent of wind
and appears to be laughing,
tickled by thunder."

NOTE OF LOVE
(to my bride of 57 years).

I speak to you, one to one,
while greeting you
as a shadow greets a sun
while warming
next to a borrowed ray,
while waiting
to be overshadowed
by the darkness
silently ambuscading light.

I do not contrast your grace
with terrestrial things
sought to be possessed
or with possessions possessed
by owners who act for sake
of spiced ownership.
No. Not that.

Rather I speak of you,
brilliantly colored
in a color-palette of browns,
a living enhancement to life,
being you as you are –
continuous,
rapturous
notes
of beauty
and love.

MAGIC AND MYSTERY OF BETTY.

It takes so little to make her happy!

Bright beams of light
through the kitchen window;
shadows on a wall;

faces of nature reflected
as pictures in puddles of rain water;

a bird that sings when she whistles;

a sunrise and a sunset;
snow, rain, and the moon in a fog;
green grass; autumn leaves
in colors in trees;

a smile in her direction;
the sound of a blue note in jazz
or the blues;

goat cheese, organic baby spinach,
and tomato warmed on dark bread;

any pleasant news;
a friend's good fortune;
the splendor and the humor
in everyone, in everything;
a rainbow in every day –

the magic and mystery of Betty.

YOUNG DAUGHTER.

You believe: Nothing can ever mean
what he meant or be as he seemed;
you can never laugh as you laughed
or dream as you dreamed.
With love, you are finished;
you have had your fill.
Know: Love will live again
when you love again,
and you will.

THANK YOU, ALICE.

Your text stated,
"I am terminally ill;
it is incurable."

Immediately, I called.
You answered, "I am dying.
Try not to be too sad."

Angry and in despair,
I reacted, "I will not be sad
when you give me better news!"

At that, you laughed,
causing me to smile
as you died
laughing.

Thank you, Alice.

WHO AM I?

Why reach out and grab the air.
open your hand; I am there.
Now blow and watch me go.
I am the happiness in that face
and the savagery in every race,
the color in the skin
of that immediate man,
the defiant who stood
and the diffident who ran.

Who am I?
Why, the dry cry, the smile,
the curse, the truth, the lie.
I am the holes you dig,
and what you plant,
and the dirt you cast aside;
that and the hurt of that
which feels but must divide.

Who am I?
Why, the moving lips, the word,
the image, the miracle, the book.
I am that in every mirror
waiting for a look.

PAIN BANGS THE DRUM.

Pain
raps, taps, beats, bangs
with drumsticks of bone,
painstakingly performs
tours of inexorable pain
in continuous rhythms of pain
through the tenses of time,
in the base unit of a second,
sixty (60) seconds
every minute,
onto a drum of living tissue,
my body.

Pain, pain
raps, taps, beats, bangs
with drumsticks of bone
painstakingly performs
tours of inexorable pain
in continuous rhythms of pain
through the tenses of time
in the base unit of a second,
every second,
sixty (60) seconds
every minute,
three thousand sixty hundred (3,600) seconds
every hour,
onto a drum of living tissue,
my body.

Pain, pain, pain
raps, taps, beats, bangs
with drumsticks of bone

painstakingly performs
tours of inexorable pain
in continuous rhythms of pain
through the tenses of time
in the base unit of a second,
every second,
sixty (60) seconds
every minute,
three thousand sixty hundred (3,600) seconds
every hour,
eighty-six thousand four hundred (86,400) seconds
every day,
onto a drum of living tissue,
my body.

Pain, pain, pain, pain
raps, taps, beats, bangs
with drumsticks of bone
painstakingly performs
tours of inexorable pain
in continuous rhythms of pain
through the tenses of time,
every second,
every minute,
every hour,
every day
onto a drum of living tissue,
my body.

Pain raps! Pain taps! Pain beats! Pain bangs!
With drumsticks of bone
onto a drum of living tissue,
my body.

PICTURE-PERFECT.

I tiptoe through existence
and endeavor to go unnoticed
by both the living and the dead.
I wager survival in a gamble
with life. To increase my odds,
I look the other way, take the other side,
use the other door, bear a smile,
wear pants with no pockets
wherein options could hide.
I carry a small, brown, paper bag;
say, "Excuse me" and "Thank you"
and "Please" when bumped,
detained, and denied.
I am picture-perfect.

X = Y.

X = Y is not equivalent.
X does not equal Y,
and Y does not equal X
without quantification.

A value of X may be equal
to a value of Y, and the antithesis.

X = Y, transitively related,
give thought algebraic denomination.

When X = Y,
and X = fear and Y = freedom,
then (X = fear) = (Y = freedom),
and X = Y is directly proportional.

When X = 1/Y,
and X = fear and 1/Y = freedom,
and (X = fear) = (1/Y = freedom),
then X = 1/Y is a constant of proportionality
and fear is inversely proportional to freedom..

When X = (lack-of-fear)
and (Y = (free-to),
and (X = [lack-of-fear]) = (Y = [free-to])
then X = Y is directly proportional,
and (free-to) = (lack-of-fear-of).

Therefore, when X and Y
express terms of fear and freedom,
X = Y give
a dynamic dynamism

of a face to a value
and a value to a feeling.

THANK YOU, WHITE SCHOOL CHILDREN.

My head is full of fun! Fifth grade!
A new year of new education,
new through, and new imagination.

Careful! I dare not smile or show joy
when I receive the school books
being handed out by the furious
teacher referring sarcastically
to the heavily-used, second-hand
school books from the white schools
as "new" school books.

With expectation,
I open my "new" arithmetic book.
I find what I expect:
Answers torn from the book
and replaced by a neatly printed note,
"Guess what the answers are, nigger."

In anticipation,
I open my "new" geography book.
I find what I anticipate:
Pictures ripped from the book
and replaced by a note
scribbled in black crayon,
"Guess what the places look like, nigger."

Guess what. Using my "new" books,
guess is what I did all school year.
I conceived new answers;
I imagined new places;
A year of new guesses.
A year of new visions.

My head is full of new
conceptions and perceptions.

"Thank you, white school children."

THE BLUES.

The sermon scolds, incites fear
about the brevity of being,
and equates the doctrine of salvation
and deliverance from eternal damnation
with the submission of an application
to a friendly loan officer
in the bank of life, ready to lend
any number of tomorrows
at the prime prayer-rate.

The choir sings.
Rhythms rock the Promised
with promises of "Now" and "Hereafter."
The melancholy melody of the choir's
cadenced, pulsating, blue notes
dominates the faithful.
The congregation choruses chords,
chokes on dissonant divinations,
and becomes blue
singing the blues.

DEBUT.

The last scene of the last act
of the play portrays the new actor
performing a dramatic epilog
in a stage performance
of artistic intensity.
The actor breaks the fourth wall,
delivers a narration of rescue,
and urgently tugs at the ripcord
of the parachute of appreciation
as the final curtain silently drops.
Sound waves of polite applause
flow through the theater
but fails to stop or to slow
the rapid free-fall
of the play
from relevance
into apathy.

EXORCISM.
(a night club scene).

MAITRE D.
"Good evening, Sir. One alone?
We are crowded tonight.
No table's available. Perhaps
the first bar chair next to the lady."

HERO.
"Yes. The first bar chair will do.

"Good evening, Lady. Lady,
good evening. Your frown solidifies
your feeling, annoyance with my interruption,
and your preference for the privacy
of a social wall of silence between us.
It is your right, and you are right
to be here, to freely exist
in your reality, free
to be let alone to be alone.
Your posture questions
my right to be here.

"The space between us
expands avidly, very real, very apparent;
it extends beyond actual dimensional space
and separates that for which one looks
from that at which one looks.
The two looks are synonymous.
You see that for which you do not look,
and you do not see that for which you look.

50

"We arrived here separately
and are together separately
in separate aberrations.
Let's banish our separatism
in a rite of friendship."

HEROINE.
"Let's farther separate
and banish your apparition
in a ritual of exorcism.

"Tonight is Friday,
Friday the 13th.
You lack social and moral right
to be seen in public sight;
you have a blood covenant
with convents and covens.
I know who you are."

OLD WOMAN PEDDLER.
"Flowers! Flowers! Bouquets!
Yellow! Purple! And red! Flowers!"

MAITRE D.
"Good evening, Sir. One, alone?
We are crowded tonight.
No table's available. Perhaps
the first bar chair next to the lady."

HERO.
"Yes. The first bar chair will do."

VENEER.

Through this window,
I saw sunrise release this day.
I stood and marveled here. Unseen,
I seemed safe, separated, and shielded
by framed panes of glass
through which I peeked
at people linking with life
in dialogues of daylight
until a fly flew freely
through my window pass me
and into my sanctuary.
I raised my hand and found
a glassless window
framing panes of air.

Through this window,
I stare into this night
unwraped by sunset.
Unseen, separated, and screened
by panels of bordered black air,
I do not know what
flies freely pass me
and into my sanctuary
of vulnerability.

SOUND.

Sound:
Someone sings;
someone screams;
someone yells, calls, laughs.
Sound of people
animates me.

Sound:
Something squeaks;
something crashes;
something rings, bangs, and clangs.
Sound in things
exploits me.

Sound:
Before and after;
now and then;
past and present.
Sound in time
perpetuates me.

Sound:
Far and near,
here and there,
somewhere and everywhere.
Sound in spaces
displaces me.

Sound:
Fast and slow;
simple and complex;
high and low.

Sound in music
consigns earworms
to perform in me.

Sound:
Rain and hail;
lightning and thunder;
wind and gale.
Sound in weather
gauges me.

My sound:
Footfall of my footsteps;
tone of my voice;
timbre in my laugh.
My sound identifies me
and evokes visible-invisibility:
As I walk by,
Rahsaan Roland Kirk
hails me, "Hi, Felix."

HANDSHAKE.

Impromptu and ascending from habit
in the custom of a conduct of a greeting,
my hand clasps the hand of another.
My hand gesticulates; my probing fingers
tighten and release. Momentarily,
my hand hesitates in indecision
of withdrawal. Evacuating hastily,
my hand empties,
leave an immediate void
in salutation.

This time, as every time,
this handshake is as a first,
rushed into then realized
to be an avoidable exorcism.

MEASUREMENTS OF INSANITY.

This measured space
this calculated place,
this rectangular cuboid
of four walls, a ceiling, and a floor.
The congruent floor and ceiling meet
the congruent opposing walls.
Pairs of congruent parallel lines
connect pairs of internal right angles
to form six four-sided rectangles
that converge into twenty-four right angles,
enclosing this space
within two thousand and one hundred sixty
degrees of corners.

Painted congruent diagonals
divide the ceiling into
four isosceles triangles,
twelve internal angles
(ten acute angles
and two obtuse angles).

A yellow lamp-shade
forms a perigon and directs
luminescent obtuse angles
around the lamp-pole.
Windows, objects, and things
in open and closed shapes with lines –
intersecting and perpendicular lines,
transversal and parallel lines –
form angles (right and acute angles,
obtuse and reflex angles, straight,
vertical, and complete angles,

interior, alternative, and exterior angles)
postulated in adjacent and consecutive,
corresponding and complemental,
coterminal, supplemental,
and explemental positions,
positioned with me
in this green box
with the green
rectangular door.
The metal hinges of
the partially-opened door
bend into shiny acute angles
in degrees inversely proportionate
to the opposing reflex angle of edges
and complete the measurement
of this psychosomatic space
with the delusional freedom
of the unlocked, ajar, green door,
a portal of escape into the freedom
of the enclosed, locked,
green ward
in this enclosed, locked,
green prison
of this enclosed, locked
green lunacy asylum.

PSYCHOSYSTEMATICS.

Psychosystematics
systemize the idiosyncratic
precepts I forge into percepts
to lock and unlock
the mechanism of my autism,
subject my autistic
subjectivities to my subjugation,
and immunize my behavior
from compulsory
autistic connotation.

My approach is positional.
The nanosecond the traffic signal
changes from red to green,
strangers in cars behind me
make demands and submit claims
in honks, toots, and beeps of horns.
Momentarily, I command; I am in-front.
I am polite to strangers outback
who try to manipulate me
with the blowing of a horn.
Where I am is where there is.

My attitude is positional.
Placed in a net, the physical
is represented by a series of lines
and angles in a nomenclature
of geographic classifications
and evolve into a way of thinking
of a world in measured pieces.
In that world, I find
where I am is where there is.

There is an inside
to this outside.
There is an outside
to this inside.
Outside there
is there on that side.
Inside here
is here on this side.
Outside here
is here on this side.
Inside there
is there on that side.
Where I am is where there is.

There is an "an I,"
where there is an "another."
An "an I" is an "another" to every an "another.
An "an I" is always an "an I"
when an "an I" is not an "another."
An "another" is an "another" to every an "an I."
An "another" is always an "another"
when an "another" is not an "an I."
I am an "an I" whenever I am not an "another."
I am an "another" whenever I am not an "an I."
Where I am is where there is.

My interpretation is positional.
An occurrence occurs in sterility
until I infuse fertility to fact.
I identify ideologically
(rather than preferentially);
I apply a personal definition:
vulnerability, capability, ability,
stumbling block, stepping stone,
ally, enemy, friend. The facts

assume my idealistic ideas.
Where I am is where there is.

My experience is positional.
Sight, touch, hearing, smell, and taste
I convert into information.
Information I replicate, duplicate,
and automate into experiences.
Experiences I merge into knowledge.
Knowledge I calculate
into formulae of destinations
and solve the equation of destiny.
Where I am is where there is.

My Motive is positional.
Motive divides gesture
from effort and measures
the power of action.
Power of motive guides action
into loops, circles, and turns.
Power of motive launches action
into orbits of cosmic alternatives.
Where I am is where there is.

My essence is positional –
existent,
coexistent,
and nonexistent
seamlessly.
Where I am is where there is.

THE DEBT.

Blinded
by the dust disturbed
from a **traumatic** feeling
tearing rashly through thought,
the distressed mind hunts insight.
Reflection and fantasy dance
in a choreography of emotions.
Passion delivers a debt
from an inauguration
of origination.
Yours? Mine?
Ours now.

V ACTS: ALONE, LONELY, AND WAITING.

Act I. Young and free, I live alone in comfortable, exciting, stimulating space. Friends, invited and expected (and uninvited and unexpected) come to my space; some with gifts of wine or food; most without – it doesn't matter. For hours, we eat, drink, frolic, joke with each other, trade opinions, and argue social mores and politics. We are unafraid of life. We are life.

Act II. Betty and I are married with children and live in this comfortable, exciting, and stimulating space. Friends, married with children, invited and expected (and uninvited and unexpected) come into our space on weekends and holidays; some with gifts of drink or food; some without – it doesn't matter. For a pair of hours, we talk, trade opinions, argue the changing social mores of youth, and discuss jobs and education while the children play. We are concerned about life. We created life. We are busy with life, rearing life and living life.

Act III. Betty and I without children live in comfortable, exciting, and stimulating space. A few friends who live reasonably nearby come to visit. The visits are not very long. Some bring gifts. Most do. It doesn't matter. We joke a bit with each other, trade opinions, argue the changing social mores of the world and politics. We created life. We reared life. We are living life. We are concerned about all life.

Act IV. Just the two of us, Betty and I live in comfortable, exciting, and stimulating space. Children, relatives, friends, and strangers telephone, text, fax, skype, and email. When not out of the country, or traveling, or otherwise busy with her career, our daughter, Felice, stays in our space with us on the weekend. Our sons, Felix R. and Julien X, with their family, live some distance away. We live quietly. We argue (seldom) just to assert independence. We joke and talk with each other about and to our children and grandchild, each of whom Betty calls, "My Sweet." We respect the preciousness of all life. We are alive and thankful for the gift of life.

Act V. Betty and Felice are in San Jose for Betty's performance of poetry, "The Written Word," her lyrics written to the music of John Coltrane's *Giant Steps,* and Rahsaan Roland Kirk's *Theme for The Eulipions,* in the Rahsaanathon, an annual, commemorative, jazz festival honoring Rahsaan Roland Kirk. I am alone in this comfortable, exciting, and stimulating space we share. I invite a friend over. He brings a gift of sweets (not allowed to drink wine). We enjoy our company for a few minutes. Both being veterans (he, Air Force; I, Army), I ask, "What do think of Commander President Trump?" My friend smiles, sits up in straight in his chair, and begins our discussion. Shortly, his bored, relative caretaker stands and declares, "Medicine-time," "Nap-time," and "Don't want to tire him out." My friend must leave; I hope not forever. There are so few friends alive. I am thankful we had a chance to taste the gift and comment about politics. We say "Thank-you's" and "Goodbye's." As he leaves, we touch hands, and he asks, "How are you alone here without Betty?" I answer: "Living with knowledge of inevitable death, I live in preparation for giving up this space. Without Betty, I am alone, lonely, and waiting." He nods and is gone. We are alive, living in wonderment of and reverence for life.

A BETTER PLACE.

If I am not here when you get back,
know that I was ambivalent about death.
I should so like to believe
that the living I knew who died
is frolicking around happily
in a "better place."
My "better place"
is with you, the children,
grandchild, family, and friends,
wherever that place is.

Please. Keep your faith.
Do not give it away,
misplace, or lose it;
it completes you;
it endears you to me
and to all who meet you.

If I am not here when you get back,
know that I left my "better place,"
you.

CONTRACLOCKWISE.

Out of birth came being born,
but not in a beginning;
living, but not in an essence;
dying, but not in an ending.

Out of a stumble
over a rip in oblivion
and the fall
between
two eternities,
came awareness
of everything
in each thing
and nothing
in all things.

Made in the USA
Middletown, DE
30 September 2017